AESTHETICS LESSON

AESTHETICS LESSON

Christopher Doda

Mansfield Press

Library and Archives Canada Cataloguing in Publication

Doda, Christopher, 1971-
    Aesthetics lesson / Christopher Doda.

Poems.
ISBN 10 : 1-894469-35-6
ISBN 13 : 978-1-894469-35-7
    I. Title.

PS8557.O2245A64 2007   C811'.6   C2007-906018-8

Design: Mansfield Creative
Cover Image: From *Explicatio tabularum anatomicarum* Bartholomæi Eustachii.
Published by Leidæ Batavorum [Leiden] : Apud J.A. Langerak et J. & H. Verbeek,
1744. Courtesy of Thomas Fisher Rare Book Library

The publication of *Aesthetics Lesson*
has been generously supported by
the Canada Council for the Arts and
the Ontario Arts Council.

ONTARIO ARTS COUNCIL
CONSEIL DES ARTS DE L'ONTARIO

Canada Council
for the Arts

Conseil des Arts
du Canada

Mansfield Press Inc.
25 Mansfield Avenue, Toronto, Ontario, Canada M6J 2A9
Publisher: Denis De Klerck
www.mansfieldpress.net

For
Priscila

Table of Contents

SLEEPING BEAUTY

Aesthetics Lesson – 13
Marriage Bed I – 14
Marriage Bed II – 15
Marriage Bed III – 16
Naked Poem – 17
Personality Test – 18
The Second Law of Thermodynamics – 19
Seven-Year Itch – 20
The Echo of You – 21
Odi et Amo – 22
Ode to Joy – 23

AESTHETICS LESSON

I   It starts with the germ of a thought – 29
II   Poetry is truth beyond logic, Latin, or manifestos – 31
III   The photographer's shadow looms long – 33
IV   If I believed in the soul, I would, by rules of logic – 35
V   To a civilized pornocracy like ours – 37
VI   Every language has infinite potentiality – 39
VII   I spy with my little eye, my evil eye, my worm eye – 41

DARK-EYED PUPIL

First Circle – 47
Campaign vs. Moral Blindness – 48
Ask Not for Whom the Siren Wails – 51
For Czesław Miłosz – 52
Gielgud's Death Scenes – 54
Fixin' to Die – 56
Identity Theft – 58
Archaeology – 59
Parade – 60
Doda's Wager – 62
Consider This: – 63

Notes and Acknowledgements – 65

Today Necessity is master, and bends a degraded humanity beneath its tyrannous yoke. Utility is the great idol of the age, to which all powers must do service and all talents swear allegiance. In these clumsy scales the spiritual service of Art has no weight; deprived of all encouragement, she flees from the noisy mart of our century.

Friedrich Schiller

SLEEPING BEAUTY

Aesthetics Lesson

There is a kind of beauty
  In the barren cheekbones of rock.
There is a kind of beauty
  In fingers of trees pushed into the ground.
There is a kind of beauty
  In the play of animals before they kill.
There is a kind of beauty
  In the woman sleeping beside me.

Though I want my kiss
To be her awakening
I will not,

For there are two inches
Of nothing between us

As I am as much a monastery
As she is a nunnery.

For our union would be a merger
Of the wrong kinds of beauty.

Marriage Bed I

For years I've watched
    you sleep sideways, hair
    spilled out like a trail
    of octopus ink, admired the rise
    of your hip in moonlight,
    and thought of failure.

In sleep, there's not that
    tired look or livid flush to make
    your brown eyes black; we don't
    stake my pride against your disappointment
    out of long-remembered threats
    and accusations, our hot and cold wars.

For modern man, I've come up short
    in many ways: I can't resist a drink
    and don't come home for days, read
    your email, my eye strays,
    never clean the sheets and rarely call,
    can't provide the life you deserve,
    but most damaging of all—supposed poet—
    I've failed to make your beauty immortal.

Marriage Bed II

In dreams
>   your juggernaut father rises
>   from his wheelchair
>   like a nuclear reaction
>   and slaps a fiery palm
>   across your face.

I wake
>   as you raise
>   a radioactive hand
>   to your cheek.

Marriage Bed III

Wise now in our pursuits of knowledge,
    older, not so feverish, primaeval
    in our house of many mansions
Where autumn withers against the windows,
    carries a special scent of decay
    and burning leaves across the threshold.

Naked Poem

I

Unclothed, I listen to songs about paradise
     in the overwhelming dark and await
     my mourning potential.

II

Sometimes I lurk in your full-length mirror, justified,
     newly fragile, every scar earned, and wonder
     at accidental battles suddenly lost.

III

Often I boil my awful flesh, heartbeat lodged
     in my ears like a submarine sound or sit and inhale
     a volcanic steam-room well past my due.

IV

Of course, what I have never done naked is smile.

V

Perhaps I need a complete sheath of tattoos,
     a wild epidermis circus, vast and fabulous,
     chameleon to my long historical surroundings.

VI

Leaving you is a forgetting born in the folds
     of my suit, desperate housing
     against the fields of my containment.

Personality Test

What hand are you?
She asked. It shows your personality.
You can test for the dominant.

She says it is the hand you write with,
She says it is the hand you throw with,
      It is the top hand when you clap,
      The one you use to flip pages.
      It is the hand that raises the hammer
      Or the one that reflexes against the blow.
She says it is the hand you use to masturbate.

I say it is the hand I reach for my love with
Which must make me ambidextrous.

The Second Law of Thermodynamics

It takes some time to notice anything missing
With such a subtle theft. Where she used to sleep
With her head on your chest, you wake
Alone and find your bed
Divided. One day, quite suddenly,

You notice certain things have faded
As eyes are prone to blindness,
Ears are to silence, or lust to inertia.
Her reading chair sits empty and
Where she once stood there is

A rustle of curtains. Later, you thought
It would have been right to struggle when
All the warmth in your hands became heat death because
The second law takes from us in ways that men of science or
Science-fiction never imagined, it being a description of love.

Seven-Year Itch

It is 2:05 am.
I have just finished making love.
I think.

The Echo of You

I used to see you dying
In every part of our home.
From the basement ceiling
   you hung, twirling in pieces,
   a body mobile. The kitchen
   tools ate you from hands
   to elbows as they whirred
   and buzzed with the low chuckle
   of contented machines. The bedroom
   saw you supine and rigid, giving
   birth to flowing wounds.

All those times I kneeled and listened
   to your sleeping breath
   I heard you screaming.
You screamed in the hallways,
   through the doors and windows.
The house reverberates
   with you screaming:
I do not like how you make me.
I do not like what I am becoming.

The echo of you
   returns in silent rooms:
   becoming. becoming. be
                              coming

And then you were gone.

Odi et Amo

And I am crucified daily

Upon
You
I
Am
Impaled,
Nailed:
A
Fisherman's
Mounted
Trophy.
This
Is
My
Golgatha.

Ode to Joy

Halfhearted hedonist,
I spend much of my time in search
Of a joyous occasion:

Such as the sound of ice swirled
        in the bottom of a crystal tumbler,

My hand as I unzip the back of my love's
        best silk gown,

The eight ball in the corner pocket
        after a come-from-behind four-ball run,

Writing a book widely considered "unfilmable,"

The sound of my cat's paws as they pad
        across the tiles,

Growing old unafraid,

Having no sycophants or protégés,

A fierce Sundin backhand from the bottom of the circle,

A lick of the knife and picking my teeth
        after a fine meal,

Crowd-surfing as Slayer launches
        into *Angel of Death*,

Two shimmering lines of cocaine
        on New Year's Eve,

Writing something moderately better
        than the worst of John Donne,

Delightful ache in the arms after a long day of work
        in the blistering August sun,

The history of Chinese dynasties,

The hope that my last name will someday form an adjective,

A show of mercy to the vanquished,

Kilar's *Orawa* at maximum volume
        in the early hours of morning,

The still air after the first great snowfall.

Yet I would consider giving up much of these and more,
        for a little piece of faith, to find
        a reason for Aurora Borealis, a plan
        in the spider's web, to stop
        weeping like the Buddha over *Time* magazine,
        to stop downing Paxil with bourbon, to stop
        answering 'fine' when nobody means it, to receive
        the blessing in the scorpion sting, the beautiful,
        dutiful orgasm that drives us on, to sleep
        well at night and wake before dawn, to throw
        out divinity and still know a basis for the sacred.

AESTHETICS LESSON

I

So there it is, a wise man's pronouncement:
Art is the mirror of the world, a secondary act
That gives God His grace, and Man his way,
A secondary player in his own life's play.

It starts with the germ of a thought, slithers
Around the brain like a flicker of lust in the cerebellum
That becomes the Word, pushes towards being,
Grabs the pure white Muse and sullies her dress,
Enters the world with the subtle anonymity
And sullen mood of a shapeless prophet's presentiment
Of future joy or doom. Back then every
Flutter in the mind was foreign
And came forth like a divine announcement.
So there it is, a wise man's pronouncement:

Some things are solid, some things are not.
Some things are touched, some things shriek
Against touch. Some things are flesh, some things
Are dust. Some things just fetishes, some damaged
Things wear hearts and keys, searching for locks,
And some are whole and others wholly cracked,
Waiting to fall to pieces like a well-wrought idea. Some will
Simply rust. That's the difference: some are made and some
Just are; little arguments hardened to a tract:
Art is the mirror of the world, a secondary act

That sculpts and moulds, strips warts off the face,
Airbrushes beauty marks from beauty queens, shears
Any layers of personality that lack motivation
For psychiatrist or critic. In defiance of time and wilting
Flesh, slower thoughts and death, it makes the sunset
And battlefield pristine. A fatal wound will stay
Open forever while serene Wolfe longs for the sky and his Creator,

His fleeting permanence, his statue in the Abbey. Never mind
He died screaming in a blood cascade, denied the path of glory
That gives God His grace, and Man his way

In the world as he sees it. And it's important
Not to confuse a stoic real with a loving ideal,
A shaped thing that shapes nothing recognizable,
A perfect circle, an inaccessible crown of maddeningly internal
Logic, driven to the complete, enclosed estate of its own making.
How absurd! Why would a talented fool on any given day
Gather tools and build a monument to the Word
When so well formed a crown could never fit a head,
Nor Royal Navy paint him a bay,
A secondary player in his own life's play.

II

Gather tools and build a monument to the Word
When so well formed a crown could never fit a head,
Nor Royal Navy paint him a bay,
A secondary player in his own life's play.

Poetry is truth beyond logic, Latin, or manifestos.
Poetry is truth beyond fact, or so it should be. Problems, problems:
In spite of what your government or admen
Or Pope or Imam will say, truth is a shady concept.
It works like the cracked half of an hourglass (I may
Have to abandon this school of thinking). I've heard
Truth is a dead-end thought, an empty cul-de-sac,
A No Exit Sign, a finish line. No truth in nature
Nor in God, whose exultation provokes the lonely herd,
Gather tools and build a monument to the Word,

A little book in every hotel drawer or hand of prison
Chaplain as he shuffles the long death row. O ye of little
Faith—there are no aesthetics in a foxhole—where do
You go for consolation? Philosophy, strapped to the wheel
Of whimsy fate? Not truth I hope, seeing as we've covered that.
Maybe Dawkins' halls of science where hard reason is lead
In grand procession, its head on a silver plate. Or great art?
When you have in mind a halo of floating hair,
Would you close your eyes with holy dread
When so well formed a crown could never fit a head,

But look like a bad toupee? I am not the poet
I always wanted to be: mystic. No Blakean visions
From my sight; no Yeatsian seances; I could never
Carve my initials into Yggdrasil like MacEwen did.
I don't talk to the dead. In fact, I barely talk to the living.
(Why speak to some guy over quick Chardonnay
Or high on highballs and, for now, convinced

Of his immortality when verse won't liberate
And no stabbed portrait will save him from decay,
Nor Royal Navy paint him a bay,

In spite of his wishes.) If not a mystic, I would like
To make something primal deep, as Breton did, knuckles
Sunk in the womb. Is there a more intimate word than 'womb'?
How would I know? I abandoned that neighbourhood long ago,
Never recreate, never infest a body. I wish I could operate
Like a pit crew and thrust the Word down the expressway
With simple mechanics performed at maximum efficiency.
I refuse to leave creativity to chance
Or be a man to let his life and art go astray,
A secondary player in his own life's play.

III

With simple mechanics performed at maximum efficiency.
I refuse to leave creativity to chance
Or be a man to let his life and art go astray,
A secondary player in his own life's play.

The photographer's shadow looms long
Over the feet of a beaming honeymoon
On Caribbean beach, falls on each birthday surprise
And Christmas dinner. That shadow is the subject
Of athlete's poise, model's plastic pose, and convict
Shielding his face, of every Wal-Mart family
Portrait, celebrity mug-shot and recruitment poster. It knows
That women knit saddened hearts in sorrow
Behind a smiling image of a departing battalion. Its play
With simple mechanics performed at maximum efficiency

Lowers a veil on victory's blush, the homeward
Soldier's kiss, enemy graves. Wives were made, then widows;
Twice defined in collective mind, once glowing white
Then in deepest black. Yet for both, a photographer
Had to fix a lens and hold her: aim, focus, shoot. Like they
Always say: *captured on film.* I would like to advance
An idea that in digitized days discretion's been lost.
No one need worry about difficult options,
Deciding what out of life to enhance.
I refuse to leave creativity to chance

Shall be my motto; not shoot first, delete by dozens
Later. Plying the shutter button aught to be a medium
Of intent. In reddened darkroom, an embryonic
Image starts out weak but gradually comes
Into the world. But why this angle of the wife's face?
Why this CN Tower or Grand Canyon? Why display
One Parthenon and not another? Why ask why

I'd pick a drop from the sea to preserve? Because
I cannot bear to let that one singular drop drip away
Or be a man to let his life and art go astray,

Like a bullet. Well, I'm willing to birth my seeing against
The light, X-ray of a soul's disease or ecstasy. Painless?
Never. Having one's visions held up to wide
Exposure (it makes me doubt the inherent wisdom
In my author photo) over a period of time, framing
The world to satisfaction, a lens held so habitually to the eye
Sight is forgotten. I think of myself everywhere,
Trying to see all, what used to be called the Big Picture,
But sounding back an echoing apostrophe,
A secondary player in his own life's play.

IV

Sight is forgotten. I think of myself everywhere,
Trying to see all, what used to be called the Big Picture,
But sounding back an echoing apostrophe,
A secondary player in his own life's play.

If I believed in the soul, I would, by rules of logic,
Believe travel to be good for the soul. I might also believe
That exile is bad exercise yet good for the art (just ask
Shelley). From a frosty silence at home where the Word
Lately could not speak but afar speaks wonders
In ornate hotels, morphs idea into vision. I don't care
To pretend that, most times, life is worthy of art. No matter
Where I am, I carry a hard crystal of perfection: a painter's
Brush, a chisel, a feather quill, an aggrandizing stare.
Sight is forgotten. I think of myself everywhere.

Treble whiskey in hand, from Toronto to Ottawa in ViaRail
Car 4805, I am accompanied by a very bad painting. Dull
Yellow pastiche of the rocks, trees, and water
Hurtling by the window at one hundred miles per hour,
Lifeless in pursuit of life. It is signed 'Marple '91.'
At my age, I'll go no more a'roving, scour
The country for new experience: the body can sustain the necessary
Level of passion for only so long. No wonder the Romantics
Died young, out to pursue a new, pure tinture,
Trying to see all, what used to be called the Big Picture.

Better to die before living becomes routine, as art
Will shortly follow. These days, I've grown to hate
Politics, small talk and cheap wine, among other things.
And I hate the work of 'Marple,' especially in 1991.
I hate youthful Colin Clute and his goddamn lute (always
Have) and don't give me any crap about how sixty
Is the new forty. Happily ever after is Hell and easy

Decline sets in, belief exile. Lacking time, out of ideals,
I call to the Dionysian I used to be
But sounding back an echoing apostrophe,

Perhaps the way to avoid disappointment is to step
Headfirst into the glittering silver screen or live by fiction
Where happiness and pain are cozy. Strange and merciless
How can the Word keep up with the world? It's tempting to retire
Where faith cannot doubt nor hope despair and bad
Paintings are real. But on the train, stout Monet
Saw the world swimming into a blur to be true
And acted accordingly. His future is our past.
Spinning ever faster, we'll catch up to him someday,
A secondary player in his own life's play.

V

Saw the world swimming into a blur to be true
And acted accordingly. His future is our past.
Spinning ever faster, we'll catch up to him someday,
A secondary player in his own life's play.

To a civilized pornocracy like ours, indulgence is a virtue,
Intellect a vice, and anguish a talk-show badge of honour
Forgotten when credits roll. Plugged in and tuned out,
Talk and text, everything disposable. In the event of a large-scale
Tragedy, go shopping. Let the masses (everyone's in the chattering
Classes) hold forth: the worst are most; they can and will and do
Their worst. If happy, they compete; if unhappy, they sue. I tried
To stay with those who draw strength from suffering
When hope looked like frailty, a sped-up film reel spun askew,
Saw the world swimming into a blur to be true

And thought I might shut off, just bear my own cross,
Just forget. Think about lives as PowerPoint slides or dream
In emoticons. Should I break my staff, bury
My shaping tools in the dirt? Someone else can set the type
Of horror, chisel from marble the shapes of the many
Deaths of men. Shall I say to myself: thou hast
Neither reason nor trickery left? That all the wild jigging,
One-armed juggling, long pea-shooting, pole vaulting, tightrope
Dancing was a selfish act? That someone else was the iconoclast
And acted accordingly. His future is our past.

The shark's razor teeth chewed his memory and finally him,
Modern Romantic for whom head and love were one
And everywhere a potential affair. In a civilized pornocracy
Sex is a given, compassion a luxury. Hearts are traded,
Hearts get lost, lonely hearts are beating biologically. Every
So often someone gives of a fragile heart freely
And throws the system out of order. Poets love that. Guys like

Horace, Catullus, Dante, Shakespeare, Sydney, Faludy, Neruda,
Struck a bet to say 'I love you' in the best possible way.
Spinning ever faster, we'll catch up to him someday,

And love as well as he bids us. The hint of that heart
Bestowed wakes the Muse (Damn! I have no space
For gender parity when the Eternal Feminine draws me on)
Even if it rarely happens but asks we not confuse suffering
With the victim impact statement. Suffering teaches
Its own obscene methods, the indifferent way
It operates. Its executives imagine
A closed pattern in the air like a toxic cloud
As a bureaucrat squints at the sun's dying ray,
A secondary player in his own life's play.

It operates. Its executives imagine
A closed pattern in the air like a toxic cloud
As a bureaucrat squints at the sun's dying ray,
A secondary player in his own life's play.

Every language has infinite potentiality. No legendary deed,
From slaying a dragon to walking the moon, exists
Before it's described. Neither does a simple kindness, any
Act of chaos understood before its symbol is realized.
This is poetry; poetry is not a metaphor for anybody's dead
Mother or lost virginity. It is a messenger, an engine
That should never have been allowed to propel itself.
Poetry is a mode to caress experience and live
To tell about it, a touch frontier wherein
It operates. Its executives imagine

That a poet is perpetually close to disaster.
The good ones are. For the work to survive, people like
An eventful biography: absinthe, affairs, sickness, dying
An art made easy, not a Miniver Cheevy of rhyme,
A permanent, working fixture in a beige office. Sometimes,
However, the Muse can be a real fucking bitch. I've bowed
And scraped and begged and been turned down
So often, I must be myopic. Denied an overwhelming symbolic
Code to follow: fire, roses, gyres, towers, whatever's allowed,
A closed pattern in the air like a toxic cloud

Expanding till we can't breathe in stifling
Mimetic heat. When the best parts of life
Don't fit the exact quilt of science and words,
I am humbled before the rotating aesthetics of the universe,
The human imprint on a night's darkness, yet still deplore
A universal aesthetic. Be that as it may,
My grant applications typically suffer. Unable to explain a unique

Vision in the 21st Century economic reality, I'm stuck
Before the imposing wall of a desk. I pray
As a bureaucrat squints at the sun's dying ray,

And decides whether my little book contains truth or beauty
Or wisdom. And if not there is much to be done. And Donne
Would hopefully approve of labour against prevailing opinion.
I seek a verse loud and thumping that drives along the stress,
Long lines, clean and energetic as sweet cocaine. Yes!
(Thank you Phyllis for your input.) I'll not let doubt betray
My impure ideals and force them to my chest.
I hope to add thoughtfulness to my yearning
If the Muse will relent and let me stay
A secondary player in his own life's play.

VII

My impure ideals and force them to my chest.
I hope to add thoughtfulness to my yearning
If the Muse will relent and let me stay
A secondary player in his own life's play.

I spy with my little eye, my evil eye, my worm eye,
See far-off with my eagle eye, my good eye. I see
Sideways with my hieroglyphic eye, a world grown flat
As a computer screen. I have seen what cannot be seen
Yet often miss the obvious: each of us a ledger of blind
Spots, trying to connect the dots and remain obsessed
With insight. I once thought I could; that a glass office
Tower on a half-cloud day could become a monolithic
Magritte. Bacon's torture-house mind could test
My impure ideals and force them to my chest.

In the beginning was the Word, then questions,
Then discontent: a fallen angel of light, a half-eaten
Apple (tell me if you've heard this one before) and a people
Set aside like a spoiled lab sample. Adrift with the Word
And its life-jacket Muse, we remake the world,
Are remade in turn, put fragile forms to burning
Restlessness. (Rooted in the ideal, and unlike matter,
Art can be created and destroyed; a whirling dervish
Craft demands meticulous ardour.) I am still learning.
I hope to add thoughtfulness to my yearning

And remain happily engaged to an unhappy race. When
I ruminate upon my old friend's skull, my needle eye
Before his empty eye, my grieving eye shutters, hardly
A perfect situation for a monologue recited through
The ages but without the desecrated real, the ideal
Is an unreflective reflection. I'd rather burn drossy clay
In a kiln and preserve its abnormality, sign my name

To a house of cards, blurt an ironic epic, or build
A grade-school volcano out of papier-mâché
If the Muse will relent and let me stay

Inside the magic circle a little longer and ride
My Rocinante. I vow to construct nothing precious
As art is an interaction eye, a symptom eye, a driving
Eye. Otherwise it's dead on the page or canvas
Or stage or dark cave wall. Now that form and content
Are muddied by medium, beware one who'll say
So there it is, a wise man's pronouncement:
Art is the mirror of the world, a secondary act
That gives God His grace, and Man his way,
A secondary player in his own life's play.

DARK-EYED PUPIL

First Circle

Streets slant slightly south
On turned down feet of November people.
Without jackboots to haunt them, a boy
With a premonition of karate class, a fat
Man talking fatter on a cell—*My partner*
    is a chunk of beef! Did you know that?—
A Chinese girl wheels home a difficult
Cello, an election is waged, an old woman ties
Her scarf against a St. Clair wind, and fate snakes warily
In the low firmament of an impossible, wholly real place
Where citizens await their education.

Campaign vs. Moral Blindness

Dear Friend,

Since he was five, our son Stephen has had symptoms of moral blindness: he follows along high walls groping with his hands, is satisfied with the world when debit columns add up, acts fleshless, plays with toy guns and expects to win, allows for liberal torture while claiming the high road.

Finally, after months of voicing our concerns to philosophers and talk-show hosts, I consulted the Foundation for Fighting Moral Blindness (www.ffmb.ca) and realized that this terrible condition affects many children other than Stephen. Hundreds of thousands of Canadians, it seems, are morally blind. I recently met a woman whose 15-year-old daughter told her 'those hostages had it coming' before going back to her iPod. So you can see what we're up against.

The key to beating this condition is research: for every $100 spent on health care by the federal government, only 10¢ goes to moral blindness. A cure won't come from the government, churches, or private sector; it will come from everyday people who care enough to invest in a moral future. I can assure you that your investment will be a sound one for three reasons:

a) The Foundation for Fighting Moral Blindness has an advisory team who carefully review any proposed research into moral blindness, combing it for taint, before we invest a nickel of your money.

b) The arrival of the Internet allows researchers the world over to share their experiences with the morally blind, and successes and failures in treatment, meaning less duplication and more value for your dollars.

c) There have been phenomenal breakthroughs in genetic research in the past decade. Genes are the 'recipes' that make us all unique.

We inherit genes from our parents. Researchers have found some of the genes that cause moral blindness. Our next step is to use that knowledge to find a cure.

Here are a few examples of how Foundation for Fighting Moral Blindness dollars – donations from people like you – are getting results:

— Dr. Mairead Cabellero from the Hospital for Sick Children in Toronto was part of a team that discovered the gene that causes belief in the coming Apocalypse.

— Dr. Jezebel Tripletts from the University of Calgary has discovered two genes responsible for a form of congenital stationary moral dystrophy. Her work involves the study of animal extinction and melting polar ice-caps, issues that, theoretically, concern us all.

— Dr. Milo Justice from the University of British Columbia is at the forefront of research into the molecular causes for ethical diseases. He holds a Distinguished Research Chair in Moral Degeneration, funded by Citizens Against Moral Ambiguity.

— Dr. Morrow A. Deposed of the University of Alberta has developed a revolutionary new screening test for early detection of moral atrophy resulting from ready acceptance of the Hollywood version of the issues.

— Dr. Lucrece Muff, a pediatric moralist practicing at Montreal Children's Hospital was awarded the Flinter T. Jaywalkers Chair in Moral Research, specializing in the biological imperative behind wedding rings.

I don't understand all the scientific jargon and I suspect you don't either. But I do know that the Foundation for Fighting Moral Blindness is funding some of the best research in the world, right here in Canada. Of course, we can't force anyone to care but we're trying.

I know cures will be found. I desperately want them found in time for Stephen. That may be selfish, but what else should a mother wish for? For now, we encourage Stephen to focus on what he can do, rather than on what he can't.

I encourage Stephen to find his way in the world despite his awful condition. I want him to get the best possible education, to succeed at whatever career he chooses, and to always feel good about himself. I think all parents want that for their children.

Ever since Stephen was a baby, I have literally taken thousands of photographs of him and I pray the day won't ever come when he can't enjoy them any longer.

I can think of no more precious gift than that of moral insight.

Yours sincerely,

Jewel Maddox

Thank you for your donation!

Ask Not for Whom the Siren Wails

At Pearson Airport questions
About the new plague vocabulary—
SARS, Monkeypox, Norwalk, Mad Cow, West Nile etc—
Overthrow customs, along with
The usual springtime of riot and road rage,
Overdose, car bombs, celebrity deaths,
Drag race mishaps and whatever else will conspire
To outdate this poem in three weeks.

In this cruel, clichéd season it pronounces ill-intention,
A bad omen for someone I've not met.
Shrill, it comes like a scream from the next apartment.

In a dismal bathroom, a tick in my eyes
Pricks at the sound, eats a sunspot
In my blood pupils, becomes a synonymous act
With my shaky flesh. Shaving off two days of excess
I might take brief notice of that
Heart murmur or brain cancer or damaged liver,
Or the lump on my left testicle,
At the sage-like quality of the sign,
As much a part of the city as the sickly
Green glow of the starless night sky
Where buried far in the depths of the mirror
Is an old, old man straining hard to stay alive.

For Czesław Miłosz

Intent upon all, through separate cities
We've walked our separate ways.
Built as they were on lawless plains,
Your unnamed cities are old and tall (while mine are steel
and cold) and still smell of cinder
From torched dreambooks of your people.
In days of occupations (and there are always
occupiers and countries waiting to greet them)
You built unnamed cities of light and shone
Them as far as you could. I visit
Sometimes, a traveller I flatter myself,
Though a tourist really and I have lost my guide
In the maze of unmarked cobblestone streets,
Working to figure out what grand plan holds
Them together or at least seek advice
For my own crooked architecture. In the namelessness
Of your bright, white cities, all have a place: murderers
And their mounted dead, tyrants and subjects,
The humble and humbled, artisans, poets,
Soldiers and gypsy women eyeing coins in the fountain,
The fallen and falling, lords and lorded.
You even allowed priests; I'll forgive you that
In the spirit of the occasion. In vast
Cities there is, for someone willing to seek it,
Redemption for our restless endeavours.
When hundreds of dead Russian schoolchildren
Weigh on us and Israel builds and builds its hate wall
While mad Palestinians (who never walked your type
of streets) blast themselves to bits against it and Baghdad
Glows with war staged for the sake of warlords,
Its museum rudely open, the womb of civilization
Robbed, history erased again, there might come
The slight reek of something noble
Out of which we might harness our fearsome energy

If ever allowed the chance to stand for once
And raise a tired face toward the sun.

Founding father, now with you gone,
I stand before the great open gates
Of your nameless city
And continue to implore:
Master, counsel your dark-eyed pupil.

Gielgud's Death Scenes

I

Sir John played
Each of his death scenes
As rehearsals
For a final exit.

He died as old men die,
In a circumference of film crew,
His Hamlet long behind him
With a body fit and trim.

II

A knight of loving charms,
Late in a line of fake lords
With paper fates and plastic swords,
An MGM coat of arms,

He learned about dying, the art
Of dismal infirm men
With liver spots and shaking hands
And death to crush his paper heart.

Departure may come
With a swell of a Hollywood score
As terrible calm runs to his core
And senses go numb—

There may be an urge to sing
With lips soft and moist
Over the prompting little voice
That says: Steady John, this is the real thing.

III

After he uttered his 22nd
Set of last words, he told
The BBC: "This is getting
Easier. It is becoming, to me,
Rather reflexive." However—
And this is a big however—
When the grim messenger came
With bad news, it was all
Hands held up in a well-known
Gesture of supplication: "Well, yes indeed,
I have used you countless
Times in my craft, but you see
I was only *acting*."

Fixin' to Die

– with apologies to Bukka White

For weeks now I been senseless
In every way of the word;
Fires falter inside me
And I coulda swore I heard

Silence where voices once whispered
Now shadows grow black in my eye,
The river flows on without me
And I bet I'm fixin' to die.

I felt a hand on my shoulder
And got no child that I sired.
Flies infested the churchyard
Where I'm tired and I'm tired and I'm tired.

It's a bottle of wine in the bathtub,
The cancer lamp burning my eye.
An injection to lift up my spirits
When the chart says I'm fixin' to die.

Hospital whites glow all shroud-like
After smoke fills up the room
And the smile on the face of a doctor
Has the look of the door of the tomb.

Saint Christopher's not gonna make it,
The IV bag dripped dry
And I don't need no river to tell me
That, Man, I'm fixin' to die.

There ain't nothin' left inside me
But worms crawlin' on my bones
And in casual conversation
I hear shrieks and moans

Of a tumoured birth on morphine
And seven shots of dye
And as God as my witness
He said I'm fixin' to die.

Identity Theft

The best I can hope for
At the scene of some great
Disaster, nearby when
The towers fall, is to pilfer a dead man's
Wallet or with any luck,
Once I've outlasted my stay
Those clever thieves will fold my life
Into a Zipfile and spirit it far away.

Archaeology

Our past is up and men will journey
From foreign lands with tools and theories
To pry our dusty tombs. When these
Yield just bone and simple trinkets,
Older, more legendary maps—
Surveys, they're called—will be unrolled,
A million crucifixes and video game consoles
Becoming fossils. They'll scavenge garbage like tabloid
Reporters or malicious ex-wives.

Khrushchev said 'we will bury you' and banged
His shoe. In the end, we too
Will greet our Waterloo with a clicked remote control
And go under, dreaming our bulk in the ground.

Parade

Give us your feeble, your fools,
Your fingerless workers,
Your gibbering prophets;
Give us wildmen from the Outlands
With hair and beards grown long,

Give us exiles from the City of God.

Give us the infirm risen from a bed
Clutched in a gesture like love,
Bring us the silent, the fiendishly handsome, crying
For evil in a place gone to Hell.
Embalmers we want, nurses as well,

And all who've raised weapons without hope.

Throw open asylums and missions,
Penthouses and prisons, open
The hospitals and midnight coffee shops;
Crack your genetic seeds
And let loose the half-men,

Half-lives trembling on the lip of time.

In late October our invisible army
At four in the morning on a weekday
Shall step into sight when no one is looking.
A parade!
With music and dancing and ticker-tape squirming!

Play under the first snow of the season!

In ragged concourse our march begins
With raised stumps and black-eyed Susans,
Purple heads swollen like balloons,
The occasional litter held aloft
By wheelchairs creaking the pavement.

No conductors without crutches.

Heads full of the shrapnel of senses
We move farther into the unlit night and breathe
No air in the darkening wake and forget the music
Over there, feel ourselves grow dark,
And squander the cure for leprosy.

Come, celebrate our victory.

Doda's Wager

Devout atheist, should I ever meet
God, I intend to ask Him a fairly simple
Question (perhaps accompanied by a low
17th century bow): How could You?

And if He has a good and decent answer
I'll set both feet in Hell
But at this point I'm perfectly willing
To bet that He doesn't.

Consider This:

When Noah & Co. first set sail,
There were no weavers or tanners on board.
Nor any engineers, bankers, stewards,
Stockjobbers, terrorists, or King's men,
Hunters and gatherers (probably a wise choice),
Butchers or bakers or—indeed—candlestick makers;
No folk dancers, muckrakers, or Los Angeles Lakers;
No sages or ad execs, bootblacks, slave drivers,
Bagmen, hitmen, movers and shakers, no undertakers,
Professors of anything; bureaucrats, doctors,
Technicians, restaurateurs or logicians, dentists
Or magicians; no plumbers, pilots or tailors,
No dealers, no cooks and—strangely—no sailors.

Also absent were plant managers, masseuses,
Motivational speakers, record producers,
Svengalis, lovers, seducers,
Nurses, geishas, Medusas;
No priests, no prisoners. And no gentlemen of leisure,
No psychiatrists, Popes, or librarians, podiatrists,
Tories, Whigs, or libertarians, no teachers,
Strippers, sales reps, jewellers, glass blowers, or referees,
No Sultans, no beefeaters and no one
To run the hospitality suite.

An der wern't no fahkin' poets on dere neidder.
Or so my great-grandfather tells me.

Notes and Acknowledgements

I would like to thank my family and friends, including my mother Eleanor; my siblings, Louise, James, and Donna; Tim Hanna and Tracy Carbert, Barry Callaghan and Claire Weissman Wilks, Michael Callaghan and Gabriela Campos, Halli Villegas, Rishma Dunlop and my publisher Denis De Klerck (thanks for waiting).

Also I owe a debt of gratitude to Richard Teleky for his astute editorial comments in the preparation of this manuscript.

Since the publication of *Among Ruins*, my poems have appeared in *Arc Poetry Magazine*, *Exile: The Literary Quarterly*, *Geist*, *Pagitica*, *Psychic Rotunda*, *Qwerty*, and *Variety Crossing*, as well as the anthologies *Larger Than Life* and *Body Language*. My thanks to the editors and publishers.

The composition of this book has been supported by the Ontario Arts Council through Writers' Reserve Grants by *Arc Poetry Magazine*, Guernica Editions, and Wolsak & Wynn. Many thanks to the editors and publishers.

Because I write out of the house, I would like to thank everyone at the Atlas One Café and the Regal Heights Bistro on St. Clair Ave. West in Toronto for keeping my space at their respective bars open.

The epigraph for this book is taken from Friedrich Schiller's *On the Aesthetic Education of Man in a Series of Letters*, published in 1795. The translation is by Reginald Snell.

The central section of *Aesthetics Lesson* is a suite of seven self-generating glosas and is modelled on John Donne's crown of sonnets *La Corona*.

All the 'doctors' named in *Campaign vs. Moral Blindness* sent me emails in the first week of May 2006, expressing concern for my health and the size of various parts of my anatomy and offering numerous pharmaceutical solutions to my plight.

Finally, no part of this book would have happened without the love and support of Priscila Uppal, with whom all things are possible.

Christopher Doda is a poet and an award winning critic living in Toronto. His first book of poems, *Among Ruins* (2001), was released by Mansfield Press; he is an editor at *Exile: The Literary Quarterly*.